EVERY CLOUD HAS A SILVER LINING
EVERY CLOUD HAS A SILVER LINING
EVERY CLOUD HAS A SILVER LINING
EVERY CLOUD HAS A SILVER LINING

D0426438

EVERY CLOUD HAS A SILVER LINING
EVERY CLOUD HAS A SILVER LINING
EVERY CLOUD HAS A SILVER LINING
EVERY CLOUD HAS A SILVER LINING

EVERY CLOUD HAS A SILVER LINING
EVERY CLOUD HAS A SILVER LINING
EVERY CLOUD HAS A SILVER LINING
EVERY CLOUD HAS A SILVER LINING

EVERY CLOUD HAS A SILVER LINING
EVERY CLOUD HAS A SILVER LINING
EVERY CLOUD HAS A SILVER LINING
EVERY CLOUD HAS A SILVER LINING

EVERY
CLOUD
HAS A
SILVER
LINING

EVERY
CLOUD
HAS A
SILVER
LINING

EVERY
CLOUD
HAS A
SILVER
LINING

EVERY
CLOUD
HAS A
SILVER
LINING

EVERY
CLOUD
HAS A
SILVER
LINING

EVERY
CLOUD
HAS A
SILVER
LINING

EVERY
CLOUD
HAS A
SILVER
LINING

EVERY
CLOUD
HAS A
SILVER
LINING

EVERY
CLOUD
HAS A
SILVER
LINING

summersdale

EVERY CLOUD HAS A SILVER LINING

Summersdale Publishers Ltd
46 West Street
Chichester
West Sussex
PO19 1RP
UK

www.summersdale.com

Printed and bound in the Czech Republic

ISBN: 978-1-84953-205-1

Substantial discounts on bulk quantities of Summersdale books are available to corporations, professional associations and other organisations. For details contact Summersdale Publishers by telephone: +44 (0) 1243 771107, fax: +44 (0) 1243 786300 or email: nicky@summersdale.com.

EVERY
CLOUD
HAS A
SILVER
LINING

If you're already walking on
thin ice, you might as
well dance.

Proverb

Even if you fall on
your face, you're still
moving forward.

Robert C. Gallagher

If the skies fall,
one may hope to
catch larks.

François Rabelais

I'm not afraid of storms, for
I'm learning how to sail
my ship.

Louisa May Alcott

A certain amount of
opposition is a great help
to a man. Kites rise against
and not with the wind.

John Neal

Storms make oaks
take deeper root.

George Herbert

Failure is another
stepping stone
to greatness.

Oprah Winfrey

If you don't get everything
you want, think of the things
that you don't get that you
don't want.

Oscar Wilde

I can't change the
direction of the wind but I
can adjust my sails to reach
my destination.

James Dean

Life is a shipwreck but
we must not forget to
sing in the lifeboats.

Voltaire

Life isn't about waiting
for the storm to pass;
it's about learning to
dance in the rain.

Anonymous

Perhaps our eyes need to be washed by our tears once in a while, so that we can see life with a clearer view again.

Alex Tan

If you don't think every day is a good day, just try missing one.

Cavett Robert

If we had no winter, the
spring would not be
so pleasant; if we did
not sometimes taste of
adversity, prosperity would
not be so welcome.

Anne Bradstreet

Even bees, the little
almsmen of spring bowers,
know there is richest juice in
poison-flowers.

John Keats

I am an optimist. It does not seem too much use being anything else.

Winston Churchill

When asked if my cup is half-full or half-empty my only response is that I am thankful I have a cup.

Anonymous

The misfortunes
hardest to bear
are those which
never come.

Amy Lowell

Whenever you fall,
pick something up.

Oswald Avery

A positive attitude will not solve all your problems, but it will annoy other people enough to make it worth the effort.

Herm Albright

It just wouldn't be a
picnic without
the ants.

Anonymous

The best way to cheer
yourself up is to cheer
someone else up.

Mark Twain

The darkest hour has only sixty minutes.

Morris Mandel

Since the house is on fire let
us warm ourselves.

Italian proverb

We are all in the gutter but
some of us are looking
at the stars.

Oscar Wilde

In the land of the
blind, the one-eyed
man is king.

Erasmus

An adventure is only an inconvenience rightly considered. An inconvenience is only an adventure wrongly considered.

G. K. Chesterton

Turn your face to the
sun and the shadows
fall behind you.

Maori proverb

You may not realise it when it happens, but a kick in the teeth may be the best thing in the world for you.

Walt Disney

I don't like to think
of all the misery
but of the beauty
that remains.

Anne Frank

Nothing is a waste of
time if you use the
experience wisely.

Auguste Rodin

Life is either a daring
adventure or nothing.

Helen Keller

There is no failure except in
no longer trying.

Elbert Hubbard

All great achievements require time.

Maya Angelou

To climb steep hills
requires a slow pace
at first.

William Shakespeare, *Henry VIII*

You can't be brave if you've only had wonderful things happen to you.

Mary Tyler Moore

But the man worthwhile
is the one who will smile
when everything goes
dead wrong.

Ella Wheeler Wilcox

A happy life consists
not in the absence,
but in the mastery
of hardships.

Helen Keller

There are always flowers for those who want to see them.

Henri Matisse

Positive anything is better than negative nothing.

Elbert Hubbard

I have never met
a man so ignorant
I couldn't learn
something from him.

Galileo

Empty pockets never held anyone back. Only empty heads and empty hearts can do that.

Norman Vincent Peale

Aerodynamically the
bumblebee shouldn't be able
to fly, but the bumblebee
doesn't know so it goes
flying anyway.

Mary Kay Ash

Every crowd has a
silver lining.

P. T. Barnum

Great spirits have
always encountered
violent opposition from
mediocre minds.

Albert Einstein

Dreams are renewable.
No matter what our age
or condition, there are still
untapped possibilities
within us.

Dave Turner

Become a possibilitarian.
No matter how dark
things seem or actually are,
raise your sights and see
the possibilities.

Norman Vincent Peale

It's OK to have butterflies in
your stomach. Just get them
to fly in formation.

Rob Gilbert

A man's reach should
exceed his grasp,
Or what's a heaven for?

Robert Browning,
'Andrea del Sarto'

In the middle
of difficulty lies
opportunity.

Albert Einstein

One may walk over
the highest mountain
one step at a time.

John Wanamaker

Wherever you go, no matter
what the weather, always
bring your own sunshine.

Anthony J. D'Angelo

A strong positive
attitude will create
more miracles than
any wonder drug.

Patricia Neal

There are two ways of spreading light: to be the candle or the mirror that reflects it.

Edith Wharton

One joy scatters a hundred griefs.

Chinese proverb

Having a positive mental attitude is asking how something can be done rather than saying it can't be done.

Bo Bennett

The best way of
removing negativity
is to laugh and
be joyous.

David Icke

Your attitude can take you
forward or your attitude can
take you down. The choice
is always yours!

Catherine Pulsifier

Find ecstasy in life; the
mere sense of living is
joy enough.

Emily Dickinson

Happiness is not an
ideal of reason, but
imagination.

Immanuel Kant

If you're going through hell,
keep going.

Winston Churchill

Fall seven times,
stand up eight.

Japanese proverb

Some days you're
the bug. Some days
you're the windshield.

Price Cobb

The grand essentials to happiness in this life are: something to do, something to love and something to hope for.

George Washington Burnap

Mighty oaks from little acorns grow.

Anonymous

The more we are aware
of to be grateful for, the
happier we become.

Ezra Taft Benson

The way I see it, if you want the rainbow, you gotta put up with the rain.

Dolly Parton

Those who bring
sunshine into the lives of
others cannot keep it
from themselves.

J. M. Barrie

Happiness is like a butterfly which, when pursued, is always beyond our grasp, but, if you will sit down quietly, may alight upon you.

Nathaniel Hawthorne

All the statistics in the
world can't measure
the warmth of a smile.

Chris Hart

I have found that if you love
life, life will love you back.

Arthur Rubenstein

Always laugh
when you can. It is
cheap medicine.

Lord Byron

Illusory joy is often
worth more than
genuine sorrow.

René Descartes

Mix a little foolishness with your serious plans. It is lovely to be silly at the right moment.

Horace

The robbed that
smiles, steals
something from
the thief.

William Shakespeare, *Othello*

If only we'd stop trying to be happy we could have a pretty good time.

Edith Wharton

Happiness often
sneaks in through a
door you didn't know
you left open.

John Barrymore

Every thought is a seed.
If you plant crab apples,
don't count on harvesting
Golden Delicious.

Bill Meyer

You're the
blacksmith of your
own happiness.

Swedish proverb

He who sows courtesy
reaps friendship, and
he who plants kindness
gathers love.

St Basil of Caesarea

Forget not that the
earth delights to feel
your bare feet and the
winds long to play with
your hair.

Khalil Gibran

Sometimes your joy is the source of your smile, but sometimes your smile can be the source of your joy.

Thich Nhat Hanh

If you can find a path with
no obstacles, it probably
doesn't lead anywhere.

Frank A. Clark

Stand up and walk out
of your history.

Phil McGraw

Problems are opportunities with thorns on them.

Hugh Miller

The tests of life are not meant to break you but make you.

Norman Vincent Peale

Have patience and endure:
this unhappiness will one
day be beneficial.

Ovid

Success is due less to
ability than to zeal.

Charles Buxton

No life is so hard that you
can't make it easier by the
way you take it.

Ellen Glasgow

Toughness is in the
soul and spirit, not
in muscles.

Alex Karras

Some days there
won't be a song
in your heart.
Sing anyway.

Emory Austin

The very best proof that something can be done is that someone has already done it.

Bertrand Russell

No one knows what he can
do until he tries.

Publilius Syrus

All that I can, I will.

French proverb

Whatever you think
you can or think you
can't, you are right.

Henry Ford

In three words I can sum
up everything I've learned
about life: It goes on.

Robert Frost

There is no remedy
for love but to
love more.

Henry David Thoreau

It is never too late to be
what you might have been.

George Eliot

You can have anything you want if you give up the belief you can't have it.

Robert Anthony

Attitude is a little thing that makes a big difference.

Winston Churchill

When your dreams
turn to dust, vacuum.

Desmond Tutu

You must be the change you
want to see in the world.

Mahatma Gandhi

Life isn't about finding yourself. Life is about creating yourself.

George Bernard Shaw

Work hard. Rock hard.
Eat hard. Sleep hard.
Grow big. Wear glasses
if you need 'em.

Webb Wilder

All may do what has
by man been done.

Edward Young

Sail away from the safe harbour. Catch the trade winds in your sails. Explore. Dream. Discover.

Mark Twain

If the wind will not serve,
take to the oars.

Latin proverb

The best way out is
always through.

Robert Frost

Believe with all of your heart
that you will do what you
were made to do.

Orison Swett Marden

Never give up, for that
is just the place and
time that the tide
will turn.

Harriet Beecher Stowe

You can break that big
plan into small steps
and take the first step
right away.

Indira Gandhi

When it is obvious that the goals cannot be reached, don't adjust the goals, adjust the action steps.

Confucius

Opportunity's favourite
disguise is trouble.

Frank Tyger

There's a saying among prospectors: 'Go out looking for one thing and that's all you'll ever find.'

Robert J. Flaherty

The best way to make your
dreams come true is to
wake up.

Paul Valéry

Life shrinks or
expands in proportion
to one's courage.

Anaïs Nin

No problem can
withstand the assault
of sustained thinking.

Voltaire

If you don't like something, change it; if you can't change it, change the way you think about it.

Mary Engelbreit

Think big thoughts but relish
small pleasures.

H. Jackson Brown Jr

Be happy. It's one way
of being wise.

Colette

Being in a good frame
of mind helps one
keep in the picture
of health.

Anonymous

Look at everything as
though you were seeing it
for the first or last time.

Betty Smith

I think, what has this day brought me, and what have I given it?

Henry Moore

Experience is the child of thought, and thought is the child of action.

Benjamin Disraeli

We are all alike
on the inside.

Mark Twain

If you call a thing bad you do little, if you call a thing good you do much.

Johann Wolfgang von Goethe

The power of
imagination makes
us infinite.

John Muir

How far that little
candle throws his beams!
So shines a good deed in a
naughty world.

William Shakespeare,
The Merchant of Venice

Keep a green tree
in your heart and
perhaps a singing bird
will come.

Chinese proverb

Nobody can go back and
start a new beginning, but
anyone can start today and
make a new ending.

Maria Robinson

There are exactly as many
special occasions in life as
we choose to celebrate.

Robert Brault

Defeat is not bitter unless you swallow it.

Joe Clark

If we take the good
we find, asking
no questions, we
shall have heaping
measures.

Ralph Waldo Emerson

Be glad of life because it gives you the chance to love, to work, to play and to look up at the stars.

Henry van Dyke

Anywhere you go liking everyone, everyone will be likeable.

Mignon McLaughlin

Too much of a
good thing can
be wonderful.

Mae West

To me, every hour of the day
and night is an unspeakably
perfect miracle.

Walt Whitman

One day is worth a
thousand tomorrows.

Benjamin Franklin

Angels can fly
because they take
themselves lightly.

G. K. Chesterton

If you judge people you
have no time to love them.

Mother Teresa

What seems to us as bitter
trials are often blessings
in disguise.

Oscar Wilde

Do something
wonderful, people may
imitate it.

Albert Schweitzer

Don't get your knickers in a
knot. Nothing is solved and
it just makes you walk funny.

Kathryn Carpenter

Heaven is under our feet as well as over our heads.

Henry David Thoreau

Hope is like the sun, which
as we travel behind it, casts
the shadow of our burden
behind us.

Samuel Smiles

Let the rain beat upon
your head with silver
liquid drops,
Let the rain sing you
a lullaby.

Langston Hughes,
'April Rain Song'

Don't fear change. It's
always for the best.

Richard Bach

Do not follow where the path may lead. Go instead where there is no path and leave a trail.

Harold R. McAlindon

If your actions inspire
others to dream more,
learn more, do more
and become more,
you are a leader.

John Quincy Adams

It was a high counsel that I once heard given to a young person, 'always do what you are afraid to do.'

Ralph Waldo Emerson

Try not to become a
man of success but a
man of value.

Albert Einstein

Perseverance is failing
nineteen times and
succeeding the twentieth.

Julie Andrews

KEEP
CALM
AND
DRINK
UP

KEEP CALM AND DRINK UP

£4.99

ISBN: 978 1 84953 102 3

*'In victory, you deserve champagne;
in defeat, you need it.'*

Napoleon Bonaparte

BAD ADVICE FOR GOOD PEOPLE

Keep Calm and Carry On, a World War Two government poster, struck a chord in recent difficult times when a stiff upper lip and optimistic energy were needed again. But in the long run it's a stiff drink and flowing spirits that keep us all going.

Here's a book packed with proverbs and quotations showing the wisdom to be found at the bottom of the glass.

NOW
PANIC
AND
FREAK
OUT

NOW PANIC AND FREAK OUT

£4.99

ISBN: 978 1 84953 103 0

'*We experience moments absolutely free from worry. These brief respites are called panic.*'

Cullen Hightower

BAD ADVICE FOR GOOD PEOPLE

Keep Calm and Carry On is all very well, but life just isn't that simple. Let's own up and face facts: we're getting older, the politicians are not getting any wiser, and the world's going to hell in a handbasket.

It's time to panic.

Here's a book packed with quotations proving that keeping calm is simply not an option.

www.summersdale.com

EVERY CLOUD HAS A SILVER LINING

EVERY CLOUD HAS A SILVER LINING

EVERY CLOUD HAS A SILVER LINING

EVERY CLOUD HAS A SILVER LINING

EVERY CLOUD HAS A SILVER LINING

EVERY CLOUD HAS A SILVER LINING

EVERY CLOUD HAS A SILVER LINING

EVERY CLOUD HAS A SILVER LINING

EVERY CLOUD HAS A SILVER LINING

EVERY CLOUD HAS A SILVER LINING

EVERY CLOUD HAS A SILVER LINING

EVERY CLOUD HAS A SILVER LINING

EVERY CLOUD HAS A SILVER LINING

EVERY CLOUD HAS A SILVER LINING

EVERY CLOUD HAS A SILVER LINING

EVERY CLOUD HAS A SILVER LINING